Make Play

ROCK™

TAKE OUT THE TOYS

Make Play R.O.C.K.™ – Take Out the Toys
Booklet 2
By Fern Sussman and Elaine Weitzman

© Hanen Early Language Program, 2014.

The Hanen Program, The Hanen Centre, the Parent-Child Logo and Make Play R.O.C.K. are trademarks owned by Hanen Early Language Program.

All rights reserved. No part of this booklet may be reproduced by mimeograph or by any other means without the written permission of the publisher. This booklet may not be translated, in part or in whole, without written permission from the publisher.

Library and Archives Canada
ISBN 978-0-921145-49-3

Copies of this and other booklets in the series may be ordered from the publisher:
The Hanen Centre
1075 Bay Street, Suite 515
Toronto, ON, M5S 2B1

Telephone: (416) 921-1073
Fax: (416) 921-1225
E-mail: info@hanen.org
www.hanen.org

Parts of this booklet were adapted from More Than Words®: A Parent's Guide to Building Interaction and Language Skills for Children with Autism Spectrum Disorder or Social Communication Difficulties by Fern Sussman (2012), a Hanen Centre Publication.

Photography: Tania Cannarella
Additional Photography: iStockPhoto, Fotolia, ShutterStock
Design: Matt Monaco
Editor: Andrea Lynn Koohi
Printed in Canada by Marquis Book Printing Inc.

Table of Contents

Introduction to Booklet 2: Take Out the Toys

Welcome to Booklet 2 of the Make Play R.O.C.K.™ series! *Take Out the Toys* gives you the tools to improve your child's **early toy play skills** – skills that have been shown to lead to better play and communication skills later on.

Children with ASD and other social communication challenges have difficulty with early toy play, so parents need research-based, easy-to-follow guidance for encouraging their child to develop these skills. *Take Out the Toys* contains practical ideas and many excellent examples of how to R.O.C.K. your child's early toy play, so you can go directly from reading the booklet to playing with your child, using the strategies you have just read about. Read on to find out how to make toy play with your child both playful and productive.

The power of play

Play is as essential to a child's life as eating and sleeping. Your child learns something from every play experience. When he picks up a toy train and spins its wheels, he learns that he can make things happen. When he hears you say, "That train's wheels go round and round," he discovers that objects and actions have names. And when he holds a toy stethoscope to his sister's chest, pretending to be a doctor, he has a chance to experience what it feels like to be someone else. Through play children learn about themselves and the world around them. Everything that

your child needs to learn – social skills, vocabulary, language skills and even how to solve problems – can be learned through play.

When a child has difficulty learning to play

Learning to play doesn't happen easily for all children. Children with developmental challenges such as autism spectrum disorder (ASD) and other social communication difficulties have a challenging time learning to play. It's hard for them to pay attention to and copy what other people are doing, which means that they aren't learning play skills from their parents and other children the way typically developing children do. Some children with ASD do the same single action with a toy over and over again (for example, lifting the dumper of a dump truck up and down), resulting in play that is repetitive and not very creative. Children on the autism spectrum aren't naturally flexible thinkers. That's why pretend play, which requires them to imagine a different world from the real one—for example, a world in which they are firefighters or dads—can be especially difficult for them.

When a child's play skills are not developing as expected, his opportunities for learning are limited and so are his opportunities to have fun. That's why it is important to take action early. Children with ASD and other social communication difficulties need help with play so they can develop the many skills that grow from everyday play experiences.

"Children with ASD and other social communication difficulties need help with play so they can develop the many skills that grow from everyday play experiences."

Your child's play skills

Think about how your child plays and answer the following questions:

- Does your child look like he's having fun when he plays (does he laugh and smile)?
- Does your child look at you or talk to you when he plays with a toy?
- Does your child copy what you do with toys?
- Does your child play with a variety of toys?
- Does your child play in different ways with the same toy (for example, build a tower with his blocks and pretend a block is a ball or a car)?
- Does your child like to play with other children?

If you answered "no" to any of these questions, the *Make Play R.O.C.K.* booklet series will give you the tools to help your child improve his play skills in these areas. If your child doesn't play with a variety of toys, is stuck playing the same way all the time or can't use his imagination to figure out what else he can do with his toys, he's missing out on opportunities to develop his language and thinking skills. And he's also missing out on a lot of fun when playing with you and others.

You can help your child learn to play

The good news is that you can help your child develop more advanced play skills and ensure that he has fun while he's learning. The *Make Play R.O.C.K.* booklet series offers easy, practical strategies for helping your child play in more flexible and creative ways and learn more while doing it. The strategies in *Make Play R.O.C.K.*, which are based on up-to-date research, do not involve teaching play through drills or following a prescribed curriculum. They simply enable you to build your child's play skills in all kinds of typical play activities that will be joyful and fun for you both.

What results can you expect from using the Make Play ROCK booklets?

As you start using the suggestions in *Make Play R.O.C.K.*, you should see that your child is paying more attention to you and interacting with you more often. When this happens, he will probably start copying the new play skills you show him and will begin to use his toys differently. If your child has more advanced play skills, with a little coaching from you, he will discover more creative ways to play. He will also come to realize that playing with other children can be fun once he knows what to do.

Much depends on how often you use the strategies and how much fun your child has when you and he play together. Each child is different, and some ideas will work better for your child than others. One thing is guaranteed: The more time you spend playing with your child using *Make Play R.O.C.K.* strategies, the more opportunities he'll have to learn to play and interact with you. So read on and get ready to R.O.C.K. your child's play!

"The more time you spend playing with your child using *Make Play R.O.C.K.* strategies, the more opportunities he'll have to learn to play and interact with you."

What's in the Make Play ROCK Series

Booklet 1: Plan for People Play

Plan for People Play is about helping your child play games in which he learns to take turns back and forth with you, usually without any toys. These "people games" like Row, Row, Row Your Boat and Chase help your child learn critically important turn-taking skills, which he can then transfer to other situations. This booklet helps you identify your child's stage in playing people games and describes how to set up these games so you help him take his turn in the game. There are clear guidelines for playing these games in ways that will make it easier for your child to join in more often with an action, a sound or with words. There is a section with many suggestions for people games that build on your child's preferred activities.

Booklet 2: Take Out the Toys

The *Take Out the Toys* booklet gives you the tools to help your child develop early toy play skills. This early type of play, known as functional play, is an important step on the road to developing more advanced play skills, as well as building social skills. Functional play involves playing with toys in "expected" ways, such as putting shapes into a sorter or building a tower with blocks. This booklet has a play checklist, which helps you identify how your child currently plays with toys. From there, you learn how to expand functional play skills by helping him learn to imitate new play actions using a variety of objects and toys. As your child learns to imitate new and more complex types of functional play, he is not only learning new play skills, but is building the foundation for improved language development.

Booklet 3: Put Pretending into Your Child's Play

The *Put Pretending into Your Child's Play* booklet contains some creative strategies for helping your child develop more advanced pretend play skills. This is especially important for a child who has difficulty using his imagination. Here you'll use a checklist to find your child's stage of pretending, which leads to the use of playful strategies to gently guide him to the next stage of pretend play. You will also learn which pretend play toys are best for your child at each stage of development.

A note on pronouns used in this book

To make the text of this booklet as clear as possible, and to reflect the prevalence of autism spectrum disorder in the population (approximately 3 out of 4 children affected are boys), the pronoun "he" is used when referring to the child. However, both boys and girls are featured in the examples in the booklet.

1

All About Early Toy Play

Early toy play begins with **exploratory play**, which involves infants and young children using all their senses to explore objects. Exploratory play is followed by **functional play**. When children engage in functional play, they perform "expected" actions on toys and objects, such as putting shapes into a shape sorter and stacking blocks to make a tower. In this section, you'll learn about the development of exploratory and functional play and how the play of children with ASD differs from that of typically developing children. You'll also discover just how important functional play is to the development of later communication and language skills.

The Importance of Early Toy Play for Children with Autism

Play is an activity that fuels children's learning. As children play, they actively build new knowledge by integrating what they are learning with what they already know. The more a child plays with toys, and the more, different play actions and combinations of play actions he performs on these toys, the more experiences he has on which to build his understanding of the world. So, the more a child plays, the more he learns about playing. And the more play experiences he has, the better his language and thinking skills become.

The play of children with ASD isn't as complex or creative as that of typically developing children. However, studies show that children with ASD who have better play skills at a young age, go on to have better play and language skills later on. Therefore, it is important to pay attention to the early play skills of a child on the autism spectrum and to understand the critical role parents play in building these skills. On the following pages, you will learn about the development of early play skills, which is the first step in learning how to support them.

"Studies show that children with ASD who have better play skills at a young age, go on to have better play and language skills later on."

The Development of Early Toy Play

In the earliest stages of play development, children explore objects using all their senses — by mouthing, banging, shaking and throwing them. This is known as **exploratory play**. Later, they develop **functional play**, when they use toys in expected or more conventional ways, like pushing a button to activate a toy or moving a toy car along the floor.

The way early toy play develops in children on the autism spectrum differs from that of typically developing children. Being aware of these differences will help you understand why your child plays the way he does as well as the areas in which he will need help.

Typically developing children at the exploratory stage of play

In the first stage of play, the **exploratory stage**, children perform actions on the toys and objects around them using all their senses. We call these children "explorers."

Exploratory play is seen in the first year of life, when babies use their senses to find out how objects look and feel and what actions can be done with them. At first, they perform the same actions on all toys and objects, such as looking, banging, shaking, dropping or mouthing them. Later, as they become more aware of the characteristics of different objects, they start to explore in more complex ways, such as banging two objects together or putting one object into another. The information children get through their senses when they engage in exploratory play, as well as the words their parents use in connection with their play, forms the basis for their early understanding of the physical world. Even though children aren't saying any words at the exploratory play stage, they are starting to understand how objects feel and work and the many actions that can be performed on them.

Exploratory play is gradually replaced by functional play around one year of age.

Children with ASD at the Exploratory stage of play

Very young children with ASD often explore toys in ways that differ from those of typically developing children.

Explorers with ASD:

- **spend a longer time exploring** – Children with ASD may continue with exploratory play past their second birthday. As they get older (around four or five years of age), they play in more conventional ways, so their exploratory play becomes less frequent.
- **have a strong preference for one way of exploring** – Children with ASD may explore toys in ways that seem unusual. For example, many children with ASD have a particularly sharp visual sense. They may see a beautiful pattern when they watch the wheels of a toy car go round and round. That's why, instead of pushing a toy car, they might spin the car's wheels while lying on the floor in a position that gives them a particular view of the movement. A child's reactions to the sensations around him may be so strong that it is hard for him to concentrate on anything other than his preferred way of exploring.

Typically developing children at the functional stage of play

Functional play helps children learn much more about how the world works and the physical properties of objects. They learn that objects fall down and not up, liquids can be poured, but solids can't and the size of the object affects whether or not it will fit into a container. When engaged in functional play, children learn about "cause and effect." For example, they discover that they can push a button on a toy to make a light go on or flip a switch to make music play. By seeing the effects of their actions on the toys and objects they play with, children gain a sense of control and empowerment, which motivates them to keep playing.

Functional play begins with children doing one "expected" action at a time on a toy. For example, a child might do the same single, repeated action on a car – pushing it along the floor. Soon, he uses the same play action on other similar toys, such as toy trucks and buses. As he develops, he learns to use new play actions and he performs these new actions on more and more toys.

As he develops more and more single "expected" play actions which he performs on a number of different toys, he begins to combine mutiple actions on the same toy. This leads to more complex ways of playing, allowing him to become creative in how he combines various play actions on the different toys he plays with. As the child plays, he's actively constructing new knowledge by combining new experiences with what he already knows.

All the things children learn during functional play lay a foundation for learning more complex play skills and contribute to the development of their motor, language and thinking skills.

At the **functional stage** of play, typically developing children:

- **play with toys in the expected way** – The functional player knows which play actions are expected with specific toys. For example, he knows he needs to push the buttons on an activity box to activate lights or sounds and that he needs to angle a shovel into the sand to scoop up some sand.

- **add other actions to the play** – Functional play begins with the child doing one "expected" action with a toy. In time, he learns to play in more complex ways, adding new play actions and then combining them when playing with a toy. For example, in addition to putting shapes into the shape sorter, the child may tip the container over to take the shapes out, then put them back into the sorter again. Or he may build a tower out of blocks and knock it down.

- **use words** – At the time that children become functional players, they usually begin to say single words, naming familiar people, objects and actions. When they go on to combine actions, such as

placing a car on a ramp and then pushing a lever to make it go down, children usually start to combine two words, saying things like, "Car go," and "More blocks."

- **include others in their play** — While functional play is developing, children show their social side by offering Dad a block or showing Mom what they've built.

Children with ASD at the functional stage of play

Children with ASD follow a different course in developing functional play.

They often:

- **continue to explore toys and objects** — Children on the autism spectrum don't play with toys in the expected way as early or as often as other children. Often children with ASD are more interested in how things look, feel or move than in the usual ways of playing with them.

- **learn to do a single "expected" action but have difficulty adding other actions to the play** — When they do master some functional toy play, children on the autism spectrum may stick to one action with that toy. For example, a child may repeatedly move the "dumper" of a truck up and down. One explanation for the lack of variety in these children's play may be motor-planning difficulties (that is, the child has difficulty planning the action in his mind). It's easier for some children to do one simple action over and over than it is to use a toy in a more complex way.

- **excel at building things** — Many children with ASD - perhaps because of their strong visual skills - are very good at figuring out how to build things, perhaps better than the average child. They may construct an elaborate fort made out of pillows or create a complicated route from train tracks.

- **include others in their play less often** — Children with ASD often prefer to play alone, and that means that they don't include others in their play as often as typically developing children do. You may notice that your child is so engrossed in what he's doing that he rarely looks at you or involves you in his play.

- **are silent or use unusual phrases** — Children with ASD may play silently or say things that seem unrelated to what they are doing. For example, a child might blurt out a phrase he has heard somewhere else, that has no apparent connection to what he's doing. But, chances are, what he says makes sense to him. For example, he might say, "Mr. Conductor, you lost your sparkle," when he's painting. This may sound strange, but it could be that the yellow paint he has on his brush has reminded him of something he heard Thomas the Tank Engine say about gold powder in a movie. Repeating something that he has heard somewhere else may be your child's way of starting a conversation with you.

2

Everyday Strategies to Encourage Early Toy Play

There's a lot you can do to help your child develop new or more complex play skills, but first and foremost, play time must be fun. The more a child enjoys playing with you, the more he will attend to what you do and say, and the more opportunities he will have to learn to play.

Making play time fun begins with becoming aware of the kind of play partner you are and the impact this has on your child's ability to interact and play with you. Then, you can put into practice some key strategies that will help you engage your child in a play activity and keep him engaged. These strategies are based on the simple idea of following your child's lead.

What's Your Play Style?

How you act and talk with your child when you play together has an enormous effect on how your child plays and interacts with you. The more fun your child has when he plays with you, the more open he is to learning. A lot depends on your **play style**.

Take the "What's My Play Style?" quiz below to learn more about how you play with your child.

What's My Play Style?

R = Rarely S = Sometimes U = Usually

I decide what my child will play	R	S	U
I show or tell my child what to do or say when we play	R	S	U
I let my child choose the games we play and the objects/toys we play with	R	S	U
I get on the floor when I play with my child	R	S	U
I am playful and play like a "kid" with my child	R	S	U
I watch my child play from the sidelines	R	S	U
I play rough and tumble games (like chase and tag) with my child	R	S	U
I do quiet activities with my child (like board games or shape sorters)	R	S	U
I am animated and excited when I play with my child	R	S	U
I speak softly and stay calm when I play with my child	R	S	U

The Helper or Teacher style

If you said that you usually...

- decide what your child will play
- show or tell your child what to do or say when you play

...and rarely...

- let your child choose the objects, toys or games you play
- are playful and play like a "kid" with your child

... you likely have a Helper or Teacher style. While every parent needs to be a helper or teacher some of the time, if directing the play is how you **usually** interact with your child, then he is not getting enough opportunities to explore and experience the world in ways that interest him. Playing together might not be fun. It is also likely that he doesn't get enough opportunities to show you what he *can* do – and he might be able to do far more than you expect.

The Do Not Disturb style

If you said that you...

- rarely show or tell your child what to do or say when you play
- sometimes or usually watch your child play from the sidelines

... you likely have a Do Not Disturb style, which means that you let your child play alone, perhaps because he seems uninterested in playing with you. Some children with ASD need a calming influence since they can be overstimulated by what's going on around them. When a child seems overwhelmed by the noise or excitement of an activity, the Do Not Disturb parent style might be just the right fit at that moment. While all children need some time alone when they play, they also need to learn to play with others. Children on the autism spectrum learn a great deal when their parents get down on the floor and play with them, even if they seem unhappy about it at first.

The Cheerleader style

If you said that you...

- usually decide what your child will play
- usually show or tell your child what to do or say when you play
- sometimes or usually get on the floor with your child
- sometimes or usually are playful and play like a "kid"
- sometimes or usually play rough and tumble games with your child
- sometimes or usually get very animated and get excited when you play with your child

... you likely have a Cheerleader style.

Parents with the Cheerleader style make the play exciting for their child. They are very expressive, using a loud voice and many gestures when they talk. They may get down on the floor, play rough and tumble games and get very animated. These kinds of parents are fun for children to be around.

Parents may use a Cheerleader style to encourage a child who is reluctant or passive to try something new. Some children need a very animated play partner to get them interested in playing.

However, in an effort to be a fun play partner, parents can overwhelm their child, especially one who is sensitive to loud sounds, and prevent him from playing with the things he's interested in. Being too animated, asking too many questions or giving too many directions can make your child feel pressured, making him less likely to want to play and communicate with you.

The Responsive style

If you said that you...

- usually let your child choose the games you play, as well as the objects/toys you play with
- rarely or sometimes show or tell your child what to do or say when you play
- usually get on the floor with your child
- sometimes or usually are playful and play like a "kid"
- sometimes are animated and excited when you play with your child
- sometimes speak softly and stay calm when you play with your child
- sometimes play rough and tumble games (like chase and tag) with your child
- sometimes do quiet activities with your child (like board games or shape sorters)

...you likely have a **Responsive style**. Parents with a Responsive style adapt the way they interact according to what their child is doing, feeling and communicating. They judge when to be calm and quiet, when to be the Cheerleader or somewhere in-between. They usually let their child choose what he plays and how he plays with it and they don't bombard him with questions or give a lot of directions.

Parents with a Responsive style also know that sometimes their child needs help in order to learn a new play skill. When that happens, they provide direction for a while, helping him learn something new in an enjoyable, positive way. But they continue to encourage their child to interact and play with what interests him, building learning opportunities into these interactions all the time. Parents with a Responsive style are playful and they try to make sure that play time is always fun.

Everyday Strategies to Build Your Child's Play Skills

It can be difficult to get involved in your child's play if he pays little or no attention to you when you try to play with him. However, if you are to help him develop new or more complex play skills, you need to become part of his play and show him that it is fun to play with you. That is the first and most important step.

There *are* some "tried and true" strategies that will get your child interested in playing with you. While having fun together is the first step, being involved in your child's play allows you to create many opportunities for him to learn from interacting with you and watching what you do.

The following two strategies are the key to getting involved in your child's play and having fun together:

- Observe, Wait and Listen; and
- Follow your child's lead

OWL: Observe, Wait and Listen

Owls are wise birds and each letter of the word "OWL" gives you an important tip on what to do every time you play with your child.

Observe
Wait
Listen

Observe — and be face to face

In order to get involved in your child's play, you need to see exactly what he is interested in and how he is playing. This means that you take the time to **Observe** him closely, which is easier when you and he are at the same physical level, as well as being **face to face**. When you're face to face with your child, it is much easier to see what he is interested in. It's also easier for him to look at your face. So, get down to his level. If he's playing on the floor, lie on your stomach or side; if he's standing, crouch in front of him. If he finds being face to face uncomfortable, begin by playing beside him and gradually move so you're facing him.

Dad takes the time to Observe, Wait and Listen so he can see exactly what Vincent is interested in and give him a chance to communicate.

Then, you can observe your child while he plays. Don't say or do anything. Just observe him. Notice the toys or objects he is interested in and exactly what he does with them. When you observe – really observe – you may notice things you have never noticed before. And watch for subtle attempts to interact with you. While some of his communication may be very obvious, you may need to observe closely to pick up a quick look or a soft sound.

Observing is a key strategy because it enables you to become aware of all the things your child does when he plays and interacts. Once you become aware of exactly what he is doing, you have important information to help you get involved in his play.

Wait

Waiting is another important strategy to help you be more responsive to your child. Waiting involves staying close to your child, looking interested but **not speaking**, and giving him time to choose what he plays and how he plays with it. If your child doesn't start interactions with you very often, your waiting gives him a chance to do so, which builds his confidence. It isn't easy to wait, especially when your natural instincts are to talk first or show your child how to play. But waiting is a powerful strategy that often results in a child communicating more than usual. To help you wait, try counting to 10 silently. In that time, your child is likely to do something with a toy or communicate with you and, once he does, respond immediately.

> "If your child doesn't start interactions with you very often, your waiting gives him a chance to do so, which builds his confidence."

Listen

Listen closely to your child when he is playing. That means staying quiet and not interrupting, even if you're finding it hard to understand him. This not only helps you find out what's important to him, but makes him feel important to you. Listening is also helpful when your child uses echolalia (i.e., imitates or "parrots" the words or phrases he's heard other people say.) If you listen to the tone of your child's echoes, you learn a lot about the meaning of what he's saying. For example, if you ask, "Do you want to play with the trains?" and he repeats your question *exactly* as you said it with the same upward questioning intonation, it may mean he doesn't understand you. If, however, he repeats what you say and changes the intonation as if making a statement, he's probably saying, "Yes, I want to play with the trains."

Follow your child's lead

Your child will have more fun playing with you and will learn more when you **follow his lead**. Following your child's lead means sticking with what he is interested in and attending to at that moment – and not trying to get him to attend to or play with something else. It may involve talking about what he is talking about or joining in what he is doing. It is much easier for your child to learn from you when you follow his lead because you are building on what has already captured his attention. When you follow your child's lead during play, you motivate him to keep playing and make it easier for him to pay attention to what you are doing or saying.

"When you follow your child's lead during play, you motivate him to keep playing and make it easier for him to pay attention to what you are doing or saying."

Following your child's lead helps to build a critically important skill – **joint attention**. Joint attention allows two people to communicate about or jointly attend to something outside of them, such as an object or event. For example, a child is with his Dad in a store, sitting in a shopping cart, and he drops his toy on the floor when his Dad is looking somewhere else. He needs to let Dad know that he wants his toy back. If he has developed joint attention, he will look at his Dad, look down at the toy and back at his Dad. He might point or make a sound. Then, Dad will look at where he's pointing and, realizing what has happened, give him his toy. By making sure that he and Dad are attending to the same object, the child gets his message across. It is his ability to establish joint attention that enables him to do this.

Christopher points to a picture that he likes, then looks at his Dad to share his interest. This shows he can establish joint attention.

Joint attention is important because most of our interactions involve communicating about something outside of us, whether it be what we are eating, planning to do in the future, looking at or worrying about. Joint attention is a necessary foundation for the development of language and social skills and is one of the key difficulties experienced by children with ASD. So, when you follow your child's lead during play, bear in mind that you are helping him learn to attend to both his toy *and* you, which promotes joint attention.

There are four steps to following your child's lead during play:

- Include your child's interests
- Interpret
- Imitate; and
- Comment

Include your child's interests

Including your child's interests means showing an interest in whatever interests your child – and including that in the play. Even if your child isn't actually interacting with you, you can include his interests by getting involved in what he is doing.

Including your child's interests can only happen if you first **Observe** so you know exactly what he is interested in. For example, if there are a few toy vehicles on the floor, and your child is playing only with the toy bus, you know that your chances of engaging him are better if you include the bus in your play (without taking the toy yourself!).

Make sure you are **face to face** so you can really observe your child and he can easily look at you. Once you have observed what he is interested in, find a way to include it in the play. Get your own toy (one that is the same or similar to his) and copy what he is doing (**imitating** is discussed on page 29) or join in with a playful action related to what he is doing, commenting on what you have done. For example, if your child is building a tower with blocks, add a block to his construction, commenting, "Here's one more block." Or, if he is spinning the wheels of his car, get your own car and spin the wheels, saying "Wheee!" It helps to be playful, animated and excited when you play. Use fun words, like "Wheee," "Wow!" and "Boom," that will grab your child's attention.

Dad follows Vincent's lead by adding a block to the Lego® construction.

When you include your child's interests, he will take more notice of what you are doing, building his joint attention skills. He may copy your actions, as well as take more turns back and forth with you. The result will be longer interactions, in which your child has many opportunities to learn new play skills from you.

Interpret

Interpreting is an important part of following your child's lead because it involves giving him the words for things he may be unable to communicate by himself. There are a number of situations in which you can be your child's interpreter.

- **Interpret when your child sends non-verbal messages** – When your child communicates without words (for example, he reaches for something or gives you something), treat this as you would a spoken message and respond. For example, when your child can't get a shape into the shape sorter and he hands it to you, interpret by saying, "Okay, let's put this shape into this hole over here" and help him do it by guiding his hand to the hole.
- **Interpret when your child echoes what you say** – If your child uses *echolalia* (repeats what he hears others say), interpret by saying what you think he's trying to tell you. For instance, if you ask him, "Where's your racing car?" and he repeats your question exactly as you said it, but at the same time, he shows you his racing car, you know he really wants to answer your question but can't. The best he can do is repeat what you said. It helps him when you interpret by giving him the model of what to say. For example, if he echoes "Where's your racing car?" you could say, "Here's the racing car." If your child understands your correction, he might just change what he has said and copy your model right then and there.
- **Interpret when you don't understand what your child is telling you** – If you don't understand your child because his speech isn't clear or he uses the wrong words, interpret by taking a guess at what he's trying to tell you. For example, if he says, "Stay it here," and gives you a toy, you may guess that he means, "Put it here." To help him learn to use "put" instead of "stay," interpret with the model, "Put it here" and put it in the spot you think he might have wanted.

Imitate

There is no better way to get your child's attention during toy play than by imitating his actions, sounds and words. You will also find that imitating your child gets him interested in interacting with you, leading to back and forth interactions that are great fun for you both.

Mom gets her own drum and drum stick and imitates Luke banging on the drum. He gets excited and imitates her back.

And when you imitate what your child does when he plays, he may imitate you, making imitation an enjoyable part of your interactions. This lays the foundation for using imitation to help your child learn new play skills.

> "When you imitate what your child does when he plays, he may imitate you, making imitation an enjoyable part of your interactions."

Remember that when you imitate your child's actions with a toy, you should never take his toy! Make sure you have a toy that's the same as (or similar to) his. Sometimes it won't be appropriate to imitate exactly what your child is doing with the toy. For example, if he's putting his stuffed bear in his mouth, don't imitate that! Instead, hold the bear up near your face and give it a kiss.

There's a lot more about imitation in Sections 3 and 4, which gives you specific guidance about helping your child learn to imitate more advanced forms of play.

Comment

Use comments for two purposes:

- to describe what your child is doing at the moment; and
- to respond to something your child says or does

Timing is everything! Comment on your child's actions and interests as soon as they happen. Your comment about the car won't be helpful if your child has moved on to playing with a train.

Keep what you say **short** and **simple**, but always use good grammar. For example, when your child pushes a car, instead of saying, "Drive car," make sure you add the words that make the sentence grammatical — i.e. "You're driving the car."

Your child will feel empowered if your comment includes some of the words he has used, while adding a new idea. For example, if he is building a castle and says, "Put the door here," you can say, "Okay, let's put the door here" (using your child's words) "and let's use red blocks for the door" (adding your new idea).

Follow Your Child's Lead – Strategy in Action

Dad is playing with his daughter Maria, who is three years old. She is just starting to talk, often repeating what others say (echolalia). Maria is at the functional stage of play and plays on her own most of the time. Dad has tried to get involved in her play, but hasn't had much success. If Dad is to help Maria develop more advanced play skills, he needs to get involved in her everyday play. He has to show Maria that it is more fun when he plays with her so she becomes more interested in what he says and does, setting the stage for learning new play skills.

Dad is going to make an effort to:

- Observe, Wait and Listen; and
- Follow Maria's lead

The toy Maria enjoys playing with most is the Peg Hammer Bench, which involves hammering pegs into holes on the bench so they disappear. She plays with this toy without involving Dad, even though he sits beside her and tries to tell her what to do. "Hit the green one," he says, but Maria ignores him. Being the Teacher isn't helping.

So Dad changes his tactics. He realizes that if Maria is not involving him in her play, she is not learning new play and communication skills. He also realizes that he has to make his involvement fun, building on what she likes to do.

FIRST... Dad Observes, Waits and Listens

Dad gets down on the floor so he is at Maria's physical level and they are **face to face**.

Then, he **observes** Maria carefully, not speaking or handling the toys and **waits** to see what she will do or say. He notices that she isn't actually hammering the pegs. She seems to enjoy putting them into the holes and then pulling them out. He hadn't noticed that before!

THEN... Dad follows Maria's lead

Maria is putting the pegs into the holes and then pulling them out, so Dad **includes her interests**. She has put all of the pegs back in the holes, so Dad **waits** to see if she will pull them out. As soon as she pulls one peg out, he **imitates** her by pulling a peg out, pretending that he has to pull hard, saying playfully, "Oooh! I pulled it out" as he pulls it.

Maria is surprised. She looks at him briefly. Then she looks back at the bench and pulls another peg out of a hole.

Dad **comments**, saying, "You pulled out the peg!" and then he pulls a peg out, using the same playful tone and comment he used before – "Ooooh!!! I pulled it out!" Then he **waits** again. This time, Maria looks at him briefly and then pulls out another peg and even looks quickly at Dad to see what he will do. He repeats his action and comment. She smiles.

When all the pegs are out on the floor, Dad waits for Maria to put them back into the holes. He comments as she puts each peg back, saying things like, "You're putting the peg back in the hole" and "There's another peg in the hole." Then the "pulling out the pegs" game starts again. Now Maria shows that she is having fun. She smiles as she takes her turn and she watches closely each time Dad takes his turn. She even laughs when he really exaggerates saying, "Oooooooh!!! I pulled it out!" After another few back and forth turns, Maria imitates Dad and says, "I pulled it out!" when she pulls out a peg.

NOW... Maria sees that it is more fun when Dad plays with her

This was one of the longest play interactions Dad and Maria have ever had and Maria is clearly having fun. First, Dad imitated her and then she imitated him, showing that imitation is a powerful strategy that can be used to help her learn new skills. In addition, Maria focused both on the objects (pegs) and her dad, which will build her joint attention skills.

"Dad imitated her and then she imitated him, showing that imitation is a powerful strategy that can be used to help Maria learn new skills."

In time, Dad will show Maria some new functional play actions and help her imitate them, but for now, the most important thing is that they interacted and had fun together using Maria's favourite toy. Dad has created an ideal situation for Maria to learn some new play skills.

3

Your Child's Next Steps in Early Toy Play

Once you are following your child's lead and enjoying longer play interactions with toys, you can start to plan his next play steps. In this section, you will identify your child's stage of play – exploratory or functional — and then decide on his next play step and how to help him get there.

Next Steps: Building Imitation of Play

The ability to imitate is important because it enables children to learn new skills, like play skills. Many children with ASD have difficulty imitating what others do and say, making it hard for them to learn from watching and listening to others like typically developing children do. Studies show that, when children with ASD have higher rates of imitation with objects at a young age, they have better play skills later on. This makes imitation an important avenue for building the child's ability to play.

The focus in *Take Out the Toys* is on improving your child's functional play by helping him learn to imitate a variety of functional play actions, while having enjoyable interactions with you. Building your child's ability to imitate play actions will not only help him take his next step in functional play, but should also build his joint attention skills since he has to attend both to you and to the objects you are playing with in order to imitate play actions successfully.

In this section, you will:

1) identify your child's stage of play; and
2) identify your child's next play step – this will be the step you will help him imitate

As your child's imitation skills improve, he should find it easier to imitate play actions he sees you perform, but are not directly teaching him. This will give him a bigger repertoire of play actions that he can use by himself when he is ready.

How Does Your Child Play?

To get a clear idea of how your child plays and his stage of play, fill in the checklist below.

Check the box beside the description that most closely describes how your child plays.

How My Child Plays

My child does the same actions on all toys or objects – he mouths, bangs, drops, shakes or throws whatever he plays with. ☐

- He does not play with toys in the way they were intended to be played with. For example, he bangs toy cars, blocks, spoons and toy animals on a surface.

My child does only one "expected" play action at a time on a toy ☐

- He might have a number of different "expected" single play actions that he uses on different toys, but he does not combine multiple actions on the same toy. For example, the only action he does with a toy car is to drive it along the floor. He doesn't put the car on a track or make it crash into another car.

My child combines two or more "expected" play actions on a toy(s) ☐

- He combines two or more "expected" play actions so his play is more creative. For example, he 1) puts objects into the dumper of a truck; 2) drives the truck along the floor; then 3) dumps the objects onto the floor.

If you said that your child...	Then your child is at the following stage of play...
does the same actions on all toys or objects – such as mouthing, banging, dropping, shaking or throwing them	**Exploring**
does only one "expected" play action at a time on toys	**Single Action Functional Play**
combines two or more "expected" play actions on one or more toys	**Multi-action Functional Play**

Guidelines for Deciding on Next Play Steps

There are some simple guidelines to help you choose the next step for your child and the best toys to help him imitate that step.

Next steps for Explorers

If your child is at the exploring stage...

His next play step is to:

- **imitate one functional play action**

To get your child on the road to functional play, aim to help him imitate one single "expected" action on a toy. The play step you select should be something you think he is likely to enjoy doing and, if possible, should involve an action he already performs. It also helps to use familiar toys and objects.

Options for single action functional play steps:

- **Perform an existing exploratory action on a toy/ object in the "expected" way.**

  It is likely easier for your child to start imitating an action he already does when he's exploring objects. For example, if he likes banging toys on surfaces, he may enjoy learning to imitate **banging on a drum**, which is a single action functional play step.

- **Perform a new single "expected" action play step on a familiar toy, which is currently used for exploratory play.**

  For example, if your child now mouths or bangs a ball, you can help him learn to imitate **throwing** the ball, which involves functional play. Using a familiar toy may motivate your child to try to imitate the new action.

Selecting play actions and toys to encourage single action functional play

When helping your child learn to imitate a functional play action, think about both the action you want to help him learn and the kind of toy that will motivate him to imitate the action. One way to decide on a new play action is to observe the actions your child already uses, even if they aren't used during play. For example, if your child throws his toys or his food, he will likely be interested in throwing a ball.

The following list gives you ideas for play actions your child can learn. Remember, start with actions your child already uses, and select familiar toys whenever possible. This makes it easier for your child to learn.

Action to learn: Pushing buttons or depressing a lever
Toys to use: Cause-and-effect toys that produce lights, sounds or action when the child pushes a button or a lever – for example, activity boxes, spinning toys, ramps for cars or tracks for balls.

Action to learn: Putting things into and taking them out of containers/objects
Toys to use: Large plastic coins that are inserted into slots in a cash register; spoons that can be put into cups; puzzles; beanbags that can be put or thrown into baskets or other containers; nesting blocks.

Action to learn: Connecting two or more objects
Toys to use: Blocks, Lego®; any plastic interlocking blocks; train tracks; magnetic construction toys.

Next steps for Single Action Functional Players

(One play action at a time)

There are three different levels of single action functional play, and your child's next step depends on his level.

LEVEL 1	Your child does a few single "expected" play actions on a small number of toys.
LEVEL 2	Your child does a few single "expected" play actions on many different toys.
LEVEL 3	Your child already has many different single "expected" play actions that he uses on a number of different toys.

LEVEL 1

If your child does a few single "expected" play actions on a few toys

His next play step is to:

- **imitate existing single "expected" play actions on *many* different toys**

It is important for your child to use a single functional action on many different toys. This builds his play skills and enables him to use them more flexibly. So, once you have identified his existing single play actions, find other toys on which he can **do the same action.** For example, if he can push a button on an activity box to make a light go on, he may enjoy pushing a button to activate spinning balls in a push-and-spin toy. Your goal should be for him to do this action on more than five different toys. Always make sure the toys are ones he enjoys playing with!

Selecting new toys to help your child imitate existing functional play actions

Think about the kind of toys that will motivate your child to imitate an existing action.

Toys to use for inserting objects:

shape sorters, puzzles, cash registers

Toys to use for stacking:

stacking rings, blocks of different shapes and sizes

Toys to use for pushing buttons:

any cause-and-effect toy with a button that activates the toy

Toys to use for building/assembling:

blocks, Lego®

Toys to use for driving:

cars, buses, trucks, trains, Lego® vehicles

Toys to use for emptying:

any containers can be used to empty sand when playing in a sand box or to empty water when playing in a tub filled with water

If your child does a few single "expected" play actions on many different toys

His next play step is to:

- **imitate new single "expected" play actions** – First, your child will imitate new single play actions on familiar toys. Then, later, he will imitate this new action on new toys. In this way, he will build the number of single actions as well as the number of toys he plays with.

Show your child some new play actions that you think he will enjoy doing and will find easy to imitate. The greater the variety of play actions your child has, the easier it will be for him to start to combine play actions, which is the next level of functional play. So, if your child has never used the dumper of his favourite truck, you could put a block in the dumper and show him how to dump the block by lifting the dumper. Or, if he enjoys splashing in water, he might enjoy pouring water out of containers. You will need to try out some actions and give your child a chance to get used to them.

> "The greater the variety of play actions your child has, the easier it will be for him to start to combine play actions."

LEVEL **3** **If your child already has many different single "expected" play actions that he uses on a number of different toys**

His next play step is to:

- **imitate combinations of two or more "expected" play actions – i.e. multi-action functional play**

Once your child has mastered a number of single actions and can do those actions on several toys, help him learn to combine two or more play actions. Think of an action he does often with a toy. Then think of a play action you could add to this so he learns to imitate **a sequence of actions with that toy, which includes an existing action**. For example, if he can already push a button to open a cash register, he could learn to put a plastic coin into a slot and then push a button to open the cash register where he sees the coin has fallen.

Toys with built-in multiple actions

The following are popular toys that are fun and require a combination of two or more play actions to operate them:

- a hammer and ball toy – your child has to put the ball into a hole and then hammer it to push it through the hole
- Marbleworks® (if your child is able to play safely with marbles) – your child can put the marbles in the receptacle, push the lever at the top of the tracks and then watch the marbles roll to the bottom
- trains and train tracks
- ball games (such as basketball with a low net) provide ample opportunities for your child to do more than one play action
- building toys, such as blocks, Lego®, train tracks, magnetic construction toys, and toy vehicles that have tracks or roads

Next steps for Multi-action Functional Players

If your child already combines two or more "expected" play actions...

His next play steps are to:

- imitate existing combinations of "expected" actions using different toys
- imitate some new action combinations

Imitate existing combinations of "expected" actions using different toys

To start with, it is easiest for your child to learn to imitate a sequence of actions he currently uses on a different set of toys. It's all about transferring old skills (in this case a few combined actions on a single toy) to other toys. For example, if your child places a car on top of a ramp, pushes a lever to make the car go down the ramp, then picks up the car and starts again, you can show him how to use the same action on Marbleworks®. Or, you can transfer these actions to a variety of homemade ramps, as well as add the action of driving the car along a track.

Imitate some new "expected" action combinations

If your child already has a number of play action combinations, you can introduce him to some new ones. Think of what your child enjoys doing now and see if you can use that knowledge to introduce some new play combinations that are similar to what he already does. For example, if he enjoys playing with cars and trucks on a track, he might enjoy playing with trains on a track. This might involve putting the track pieces together, then connecting the engine and a few cars and driving them along the track.

Harrison has learned to combine the actions of connecting the pieces of the train and pushing the train over the bridge.

4

R.O.C.K. Your Child's Functional Play

Now that you know your child's next play step, you are ready to help him take that step by R.O.C.K.ing his play! As you apply the R.O.C.K. strategy, you'll continue to use the everyday strategies Observe, Wait and Listen and Follow Your Child's Lead. But you'll take things a step further by showing your child a new play step and encouraging him to imitate that step. By learning to imitate play steps, your child will develop a repertoire of play actions which, in time, he can imitate easily and then use on his own with many different toys.

ROCK Your Child's Functional Play

Once you have identified your child's next functional play step, you can start to R.O.C.K. his play. The main idea of R.O.C.K. in early toy play is to make it easy and fun for your child to learn to imitate the identified play step.

R	**Repeat (imitate) your child's action/s** with toys or objects to get some back and forth interaction going; and then **Repeat the new play action** you want your child to imitate
O	**Offer opportunities** for your child to imitate the play action/s
C	**Cue** your child to imitate the play action
K	**Keep the play fun and keep it going!**

Before you can start to use R.O.C.K., you must have identified your child's next play step. So if you skipped that section, go back and read pages 36-44. This step is really what the "Offer opportunities" part of R.O.C.K. is about. Once you have a clear idea of what you are helping your child learn, this becomes his "Opportunity" and you can use R.O.C.K. to help him learn this play step.

Repeat your child's actions
– Imitate what your child does while he is playing

Repeat the new play action
– Show him the new play step and repeat it at least three times

Repeat your child's actions

When your child is playing with toys or objects, get down beside him and repeat what he does with his toys. Repeating (imitating) your child's play actions helps you gain his attention. It also makes it easier for him to imitate you back because he is motivated to repeat an action that he has already performed.

FIRST... ***Get face to face and observe*** *what your child is doing with his toys;*
Wait *to see what else he will do...; and*
Listen *closely to what he's saying.*

THEN... ***Follow his lead***

- ***Imitate his actions*** *– Always have your own toy so you never take your child's toy! (You can also imitate his sounds and words, but don't expect him to imitate these back to you).*
- ***Comment*** *on his actions or on what he says.*
- ***Wait*** *for him to imitate you back with these actions (If he imitates your sounds and words, consider it a bonus – but don't expect it).*

When your child imitates the actions you have just imitated...

- ***Repeat again – Imitate*** *his actions again (and sounds and words),* ***comment*** *and* ***wait*** *again for him to imitate the actions (again, don't expect him to imitate the sounds and words as well)*
- ***Imitate*** *each other back and forth many times.*

Repeat the new play action

Once you and your child have imitated each other back and forth a number of times, you are ready to show him the new play step.

- *Make sure you have duplicates of the toys you are going to use*
- *Put the duplicate toy in front of your child.*
- ***Model** the new play action (his next play step) three times.*
- ***Comment** on your action to draw your child's attention to it – for example, "I'm pushing the ball down the ramp" or "The ball's going fast!" You can vary what you say each time, but keep it short, simple and grammatical.*
- ***Repeat both** the play action and the comment at least three times.*

You can model two play steps during one play time, as long as they reflect the same stage of play and type of play step you identified as your child's next step.

Offer opportunities for your child to do the new play step(s)
– Before you begin the play, you should have identified your child's next play step/s so you know what you are aiming for.

Your child's next play step is his "opportunity", and you will help him take it by using **cues...**

Cue your child to do the new play step/s on his own
*– If your child doesn't imitate the new play step after you model it three times, **waiting** is always your first cue. If he needs more help, you will use a stronger cue to help him know what to do.*

Cues let your child know what to do and are an important part of helping him learn how to play. After your child has observed you perform the new play action at least three times, your first cue is to **wait** for about 10 seconds without saying anything to see if he'll imitate you. If he imitates you right away, the next time you may not need to model the play action three times. However, if demonstrating the action and then waiting is not enough, you will have to give him some **extra cues**.

Do's for extra cues

- **Only use extra cues after *waiting* for 5-10 seconds** – This important first cue lets your child know he is expected to do something.
- **Use hand over hand physical help** – Take your child's hands and move them so he performs the action with the toy.
- **Reward him enthusiastically as soon as he imitates you** (even if you have given him physical help) by telling him what he did. For example, say "Yay, you pushed the button!" or "Wow! The ball's going down the ramp!"

- **After giving your child hand over hand help many times, try a less obvious cue** – Let your child experience hand over hand help many times so he knows the play step well. You can then try to use a less obvious extra cue like a point at the object or a touch to his hand to remind him what to do. If he doesn't imitate the play step within a few seconds, go back to hand over hand help.

Don'ts for cues

- **Don't *tell* your child what to do** – For example, don't say, "Do what Mommy is doing," or "Push the button." You don't want your child to depend on a verbal instruction. The goal is for him to perform the action on his own, even if this takes longer for him to learn.
- **Don't say "Good job" or "Good boy"** – This kind of praise lets your child know you're happy, but it doesn't give him information about what he did and the effects of his play actions.
- **Don't worry if your child's imitation is not exact** – Any attempt to imitate is more important than whether it is accurate. Praise every attempt your child makes to imitate the play action and don't use cues to try to get him to improve the quality of his imitation.

Once your child has imitated the new play step – with or without a cue – let him continue to play however he wants. That means he might go back to playing as he did before you showed him the new play step. Follow his lead, imitate him and comment on what he is doing. Get some back and forth imitation going again.

About a minute or so later, show him the new play step again three times and wait for about 5 seconds to see if he will imitate you. If he does, then you need only model the play step once next time. If he doesn't imitate you, cue him with hand over hand help again, and then reward him by getting excited and saying something like, "Yay! You dumped the blocks!" If and when your child imitates the play step without any help from you, be sure to be very enthusiastic!

Your goal is for your child to imitate you without physical cues – i.e. without hand over hand help. So, aim to use less obvious cues once your child is familiar with the activity and you have given him many opportunities to receive hand over hand cues. And remember to **wait each time you model the new play step** so that, when he can imitate all by himself, you give him an opportunity to do so.

Keep the play fun and keep it going!
– Be playful! Model actions your child is likely to want to perform. Play often so he gets lots of practice.

Keep the play fun – An important part of R.O.C.K.ing your child's functional play involves making the interaction fun. The more playful you are and the more fun your child has, the more likely he is to attend to you when you show him the new play step, making it easier for him to imitate it. If your child sees imitation as a way of continuing a social interaction with you, you have set the stage for him to learn every time you play.

> "The more playful you are and the more fun your child has, the more likely he is to attend to you when you show him the new play step, making it easier to imitate the play action."

To be playful when you are with your child, use an animated tone of voice and play like a kid. Model actions you know he will find interesting and enjoyable, using toys you know he likes. When you help him imitate the new play step, show your excitement and reward him by commenting enthusiastically about what he's done. Make sure your child is still motivated to play with the toy. If he loses interest in a toy, switch to a different one.

Keep the play going – Your child needs many opportunities to imitate the new play step. Play with him as often as you can, making sure you start by imitating his play actions and following his lead. Then, model the new play action many times during the play. You can model the new play step three times every minute or two, giving him lots of opportunities to practice imitating it. Then cue him if he needs it.

Once your child is having success imitating the new play step, make sure you give him enough practice so that he can imitate the play step easily on many toys without hand over hand cues.

If ROCK doesn't work at first, Intrude

Sometimes, your child may find it really hard to stop what he is doing and pay attention to you. He may be doing something over and over again with an object and may pay no attention to you at all, even when you R.O.C.K. his play. In this case, **Intrude**. This means insisting on joining in on what your child is doing, even if he doesn't want you to. Once you persist — using one or more of the ideas below — your child will learn that it's more fun to play with you than to play alone.

Intruding can take various forms:

Being the keeper – If your child is lining things up or dropping things or rubbing them up and down his body, gather up the objects and make yourself part of the game by giving him one object at a time. At first, give the object to him saying something like, "Here's a block." But then, hold on to the object for a second and see if he will look at you or request it in some way. Or, instead of giving your child the objects you are holding one by one, give him one and then use one to take the same turn he is taking, then go back to giving him an object. For example, after you give your child a block, which he drops on the floor, you drop a block onto the floor. Then give him another block, which he drops on the floor, and then you drop another block onto the floor. In this way, you become part of the game.

Hiding and searching – If your child is very focused on an object, take it and make a game of hiding it somewhere nearby. First, get down to his physical level and imitate what he is doing. If he is rubbing an object up and down his chest, take the object and do the same thing so you get his attention. Then, intrude by hiding the toy, even though he may see where you have hidden it. Your child will have to interact with you to find the object, and the game can be a lot of fun. Make sure you are very playful, saying in a very animated way, "Where's the car?" and "Let's look under the couch!" Help him search for and find the toy, and get excited when he finds it. You may be able to turn a solo game into an interactive game by making the hiding game too much fun to ignore!

Get in the way – Sometimes, you can engage your child by getting in his way and turning getting out of the way into some kind of interaction. For example, blocking your child when he's running or when he's trying to open the toy cupboard creates the need for interaction. He will have to let you know that he wants you out of the way and, by that time, you are already part of his game. Be playful. For example, when he's running, stand in his way and hold up your hand, saying "Stop!" with a big smile on your face.

Intruding breaks the cycle of your child's difficulty with interaction and allows you to work your way into his play, even if he seems not to welcome it at first. Once you have established an interaction, you can move on to R.O.C.K.

> "Intruding breaks the cycle of your child's difficulty with interaction and allows you to work your way into his play, even if he seems not to welcome it at first."

5

Real Life Examples

Now let's look at some real-life examples. Alex and Luke's parents use the key strategies and R.O.C.K. to help their children take the next step in functional play. While the children are having fun playing with their parents, they are learning to imitate new functional play skills.

ROCKing Alex's Play:

The Explorer learns to do one functional play action with a toy

Mom identifies Alex's stage of play and she decides on his next play step. Once she has that information, she can R.O.C.K. Alex's play.

FIRST... **Mom Observes Alex to identify his stage of play:**

Alex plays with toys and objects by doing the same actions on all of them. No matter which toys or objects he's playing with, he bangs, rolls, spins or throws them. But he seems to enjoy throwing objects the most. He throws or drops both toys and other everyday objects like spoons and pieces of paper. He seems to like the feeling of flinging objects and watching where and how they land.

Alex is at **the exploring stage** of play.

SECOND... **Mom identifies Alex's next play step and the toys she needs:**

Mom decides that Alex's next play step is to **imitate one functional play action** – using an existing action she has observed in his exploratory play.

Since Alex enjoys throwing things, Mom will help him learn to use this throwing action on a toy that is used for throwing (an **"expected" action**).

The best toys and activities to help Alex take this next step: Mom chooses a toy that she knows Alex will like and that will be easy for him to throw: small, soft, coloured balls. To make it easy for him to throw the balls into a container, she will use a large laundry basket.

THEN... **Mom R.O.C.K.s Alex's play:**

Repeat Alex's actions

Alex is on the floor playing with a set of blocks. He is banging and throwing them. Mom gets down on the floor and lies on her side so she and Alex are face to face. She takes a few blocks (leaving most of them for Alex) and puts a number of the soft, coloured balls on the floor near her.

Then she **Observes**, **Waits** and **Listens**...

Alex picks up a block and throws it on the ground. He does that a few times.

Mom **follows Alex's lead**. She picks up a block and says, "I'm gonna throw the block too!" as she throws it on the ground and **waits**. Alex glances at her briefly, looking surprised. He throws another block on the ground. Mom says, "You threw the block!" and then she throws a block onto the ground, saying, "I threw my block too!"

Alex "gets" what's happening and he smiles and throws another block on the ground. Then Mom imitates him again. They go back and forth taking turns throwing the block onto the floor a number of times. Each time, Mom **comments** on what Alex is doing as well as on what she is doing.

Repeat the new play step

Once Alex and Mom have imitated each other back and forth a few times, Mom is ready to show Alex his next play step – i.e. throwing a toy that is supposed to be thrown.

Mom puts a few of the soft coloured balls in front of Alex, keeping some for herself. The next time Alex throws a block on the ground, Mom picks up a ball, holding it up so Alex can see it. She moves the laundry basket in front of her and says, "I'm gonna throw the ball into the basket!" and she does.

Mom repeats the new play step three times in a row. Each time she throws a ball into the basket, she makes a comment and shows her excitement. She says things like, "Into the basket!", "Wow!" or "The ball's in the basket!"

Offer opportunities

Mom has identified Alex's next functional play step – she is aiming for him to imitate the action of throwing a ball into the laundry basket. To help him do this, she has to make sure he knows it is his turn and how to take that turn. Cues help her do this.

Cue

Once Alex has seen Mom throw the ball into the basket three times, she cues him to take his play step by **waiting about 10 seconds, not doing anything but looking at him expectantly**. Alex throws a block on the ground again. So, Mom provides a **hand over hand cue**.

What Mom does...

- **gives hand over hand help**: She puts a ball into Alex's hand and gives him some hand over hand help, guiding him so he throws the ball into the laundry basket.
- **rewards him by telling him what he did**: Mom gets excited and says, "The ball's in the basket! Yay!" when he throws the ball into the basket with her help.
- **goes back to letting Alex play his own way**: Mom follows Alex's lead, imitating him throwing blocks onto the ground and commenting on what he's doing. She gets some back and forth imitation going again.

A minute or so later, Mom repeats the play step and throws her ball into the laundry basket. She does this three times in a row. Alex does not imitate her, so she provides cues again...

When Alex throws a block on the ground, she gives him another ball and provides hand over hand help so he throws the ball into the basket. She then rewards him by making the comment, "Wow! You threw the ball in the basket again!"

The next time Mom repeats this process, Alex imitates her and throws the ball into the basket! Starting with an existing action has made this task easier for Alex, and it is fun to throw a ball and get it into a basket!

Keep the play fun and keep it going!

Keep the play fun – Mom is playful and animated and she shows her excitement each time Alex imitates the throwing action with the ball. She watches carefully to make sure he is having fun. She notices that he looks excited as she throws the ball into the basket and that he glances at her after he imitates the throwing action so he can enjoy her enthusiastic response. She wants the interaction to remain an important part of the game and so she keeps the game exciting and motivating for Alex.

... and Keep it going

Mom can't stop now. She can keep the play going by:

- continuing to play with Alex often – inside the house and outside – giving him lots of opportunities to throw balls into the laundry basket
- involving Dad and other family members in the throwing game with Alex, as long as they stick to the R.O.C.K. process of imitating him, following his lead and having fun together — and then modelling the play step for him to imitate
- changing the container into which Alex throws the soft balls – for example, using a large cardboard box or a garbage can
- introducing other toys that can be thrown into the basket, like balls of different sizes, bean bags and soft rings
- using a toy basketball net and soft ball and helping Alex learn a well-known game

It's important for Alex to get lots of practice so he can learn to imitate this "throw balls and other objects into a container" play step easily using a number of different objects and containers. As he gets better and better at throwing games, he will be developing important functional play skills that he can use in the future during play with other people, including other children.

Mom expands Alex's ability to imitate the play step by introducing balls of different sizes.

ROCKing Luke's Play:

From many single functional play actions on many toys to combining two functional play actions on a toy

Mom will first identify Luke's stage of play and then she will identify his next play step. Once she has that information, she can R.O.C.K. his play.

FIRST... **Mom Observes Luke to identify his stage of play:**

Luke enjoys playing with puzzles and shape sorters, but what he seems to enjoy most is playing with vehicles.

Mom spends some time observing Luke's play with vehicles because she thinks there's lots of potential to build on this kind of play. He drives his cars and trucks all over the floor. He has a speedway, which is supposed to be operated by placing the cars on the loading ramp and then pushing the lever so the cars are released onto the track. However, Luke doesn't use the ramp or the lever. He puts the cars on a high point of the track and lets them go. Even though Mom has shown him how to put the car on the ramp and push the lever to release the cars, this hasn't helped him learn to do it.

Luke is at the stage of functional play where **he can do a number of single play actions on many different toys** (Single Action Functional Player, Level 3 – see page 42).

SECOND... **Mom identifies Luke's next play step and the toys she needs:**

Mom is going to help Luke **imitate a combination of two actions on a toy**, with one of the actions being an existing action (one she has seen him use in his play).

Since Luke enjoys playing with vehicles, Mom plans to use the speedway to help him combine the following play actions:

1) Put the car on the loading ramp (an existing action – in this case, he will be putting the car on a different part of the speedway using the same action of lifting the car and placing it on the toy); and then

2) Push the lever on the ramp to release the car so it runs along the track.

THEN... **Mom R.O.C.K.s Luke's play:**

Repeat Luke's actions

Luke is playing on the floor with his cars and trucks beside the speedway.

Mom **Observes, Waits and Listens.**

Mom lies on her side on the floor so she and Luke are face to face and she can observe him closely. He is playing with his cars by putting them on the track of the speedway and letting them go, making a "Vroom vroom" sound as they run down the track.

Mom **follows Luke's lead**. She gets some cars for herself and picks one up, saying, "I'm gonna put this car on the track." She **imitates** him, putting a car on the track and then letting it go. She says "Vroom Vroom" and **comments**, "Wow! Look at the car go!" and then she **waits**...

Luke watches her car run on the speedway. Then he picks up a car, puts it on the track and lets it go, making the "Vroom vroom" sound.

Mom imitates him again by saying, "Vroom, Vroom!" and commenting, "That car is going fast!" just to change things up a bit.

Luke seems to like this game and he smiles. He continues to put cars on the speedway's track, letting them run down the track and Mom follows his lead, imitating him and commenting each time. They go back and forth imitating each other a number of times.

R Repeat the new play step

Once Luke and Mom have imitated each other back and forth a number of times, Mom is ready to show Luke the next play step – **combining two actions on a toy, with one of the actions being an existing action**.

The next time Luke puts a car on the track, Mom doesn't imitate him. She puts her car on the loading ramp, saying, "The car is on the ramp. Now, I'm gonna push the lever" and then, as she pushes the lever, she says, "There goes the car!" As the car speeds down the ramp, Mom describes what's happening with lots of enthusiasm. She exclaims, "Wheee! The car's speeding down the track!"

Mom repeats the new play step combination three times in a row. Each time, she talks about what she is doing ("I'm putting the car on the loading ramp and now, I'm gonna push the lever!" or "Let's push the lever!") and when the car is released down the ramp, she makes a comment showing her excitement by saying, "Wow! There goes the car!" or "The car's speeding down the track!"

Offer opportunities

Mom has identified Luke's next play step – she is aiming for him to imitate a combination of two actions using the loading ramp and the lever. To help him do this, she has to make sure he knows it is his turn and how to take that turn. Cues help her do this.

Cue

Once Luke has seen Mom repeat the combined play steps three times, she is ready to cue him to imitate this play step. She **waits for 10 seconds, not doing anything but looking at him expectantly.**

Luke doesn't imitate her – he continues to let his cars run down the track from the loading ramp.

What Mom does...

- **gives hand over hand help**: When Luke has a car in his hand, Mom guides his hand so he puts the car onto the loading ramp, saying, "The car is on the loading ramp. Now, let's push the lever" and then she helps him push the lever so the cars run down the ramp.

- **rewards him by telling him what he did**: Mom gets excited and says, "Wow! There go the cars! Wheee!"
- **goes back to letting Luke play his own way**, following his lead, imitating whatever he does even if he isn't pushing the lever. By imitating him and commenting on what he's doing, Mom is keeping Luke interested in playing with her and getting some back and forth imitation going again.

A minute or so later, Mom repeats the combined steps three times and, when Luke doesn't imitate her, she cues again in the same way that she did before.

Mom repeats this process many times. Each time, after she has modelled the combined play steps three times, she waits for five to ten seconds to give Luke a chance to imitate her. If he doesn't, she provides hand over hand help.

Keep the play fun and keep it going!

Keep the play fun – Mom makes sure Luke is having fun. She is playful and animated and she shows her excitement by commenting enthusiastically when she cues him to imitate the combined actions on the speedway.

...and Keep it going!

Mom tries to set aside time to play with Luke every day. She continues to model the combined play steps and provide hand over hand cues. After a few days, when Mom models the combined action with the car on the speedway, Luke puts his car on the ramp instead of putting it on the track. He then tries to push the lever down, but he isn't pushing hard enough to release the car. Mom continues to give hand over hand help, showing him how to push the lever down with enough force to release the cars, saying "Yay! There goes the car!" when the car is released onto the track.

After a number of tries, Mom uses a less obvious cue — touching Luke's hand — to see if he will push the lever down without hand over hand cues. She doesn't want him to depend on hand over hand cues, so once she thinks he understands the need to push hard on the lever, she tries the pointing cue. If he doesn't push the lever hard enough with the pointing cue, she goes back to using a hand over hand cue. She doesn't tell him what to do, however. She just uses cues because she doesn't want him to depend on a verbal instruction. The goal is for him to perform the actions on his own, even if it takes longer for him to learn.

After many tries and a combination of hand over hand cues and pointing cues, Luke imitates the combined play steps all by himself! And when he does, Mom gets even more excited, saying, "Wow, look at the car go. Whee!"

After Luke imitates the combined play steps all by himself, he and Mom enjoy watching the cars run down the track.

Mom can't stop here. It's important to help Luke learn to imitate these two-step play actions easily. He needs lots of practice and she needs to stick to the process to make sure he gets all the help he needs to imitate these steps without added cues.

She can keep the play going by:

- continuing to give Luke practice with the combined play steps on the speedway
- involving other family members in the play, as long as they stick to the R.O.C.K. process of imitating him, following his lead and having fun together – and then modelling the combined play steps for him to imitate
- introducing other vehicle ramps. The choices in stores for toys with vehicles and ramps are endless, but it is easy for Mom to make her own. This could involve putting a toy car on a home-made loading ramp on the couch (such as firm, thin book) and then using a wooden spoon to push the car down a home-made ramp (which could be a large plastic tray, a baking sheet or a large piece of cardboard cut from a box). Cardboard tubes from rolls of fabric also make wonderful ramps.

Once Luke can easily imitate the combined play steps, Mom will look for other toys that require two-step actions, choosing ones that are easy to figure out just by looking at them. For example, she can introduce him to a cash register, which requires the money to be inserted into a slot and then a button to be pushed to open the cash drawer. Or she can use a household object like a salad spinner, putting a little ball into it, spinning it and then opening it and watching the ball spin around the side of the spinner. Each time she introduces a new toy, she goes back to R.O.C.K. so Luke gets all the help he needs within a fun, exciting interaction.

Looking Back

Functional play — or playing with toys the expected way — lays the foundation for the development of more advanced play skills while also building your child's social, language and thinking skills. You can help your child develop more advanced functional play skills by following the R.O.C.K. strategy. R.O.C.K. helps you structure play times with your child so he has fun, enjoys the back and forth imitation that you encourage and then learns to imitate new functional play steps. It may take time for your child to learn to imitate the play actions you show him, so keep R.O.C.K.ing, giving your child the practice he needs to succeed. By helping your child learn to imitate a variety of more and more complex functional play actions, you are not only building his imitation skills – you are building a repertoire of play skills which will increase his knowledge and understanding of the world, as well as his ability to interact with others.

It's now time to come up with your own Toy Play Plan for you and your child. On the next pages, you will find a sample plan already filled in and a plan for you to complete and use to help your child take his next functional play step.

As your child progresses through his play steps and you need more Toy Play Plans, you can easily download them through the Hanen website at www.hanen.org/toyplayplan

References

For a complete list of references, visit www.hanen.org/MakePlayROCK-references

My Child's Stage of Play and Next Steps

Refer to your child's stage of play (p.37) and then identify his next play step on this chart (see p. 38-44 for more detailed descriptions).

My child is at the following stage of play	His next play step is to...
Exploring	**Perform one functional play action** • Perform an existing exploratory action on a toy/object in the "expected" way; or • Perform a new single "expected" action play step on a familiar toy, which is currently used for exploratory play
Single Action Functional Play Level 1 My child does **a few** single "expected" play actions on a **small number** of toys	**Imitate existing single "expected" play actions on many, different toys**
Single Action Functional Play Level 2 My child does **a few** single "expected" play actions on **many** different toys	**Imitate new single play actions – first on familiar toys and, later, on new toys**
Single Action Functional Play Level 3 My child already has **many** different single "expected" play actions that he uses on a number of different toys	**Imitate combinations of two or more "expected" play actions**
Multi-action Functional Play My child **combines two or more** "expected" play actions on a toy/toys	• **imitate existing combinations of "expected" actions using different toys; or** • **imitate some new "expected" action combinations**

Sample

Alex's Toy Play Plan
(see page 57 for more detailed descriptions)

My child is at the following stage of play: Exploring

The next play step for my child is to: Imitate one functional play action

(For children at Exploring and Multi-action functional play stages)

My child will perform this play action by: Performing an existing exploratory action on a toy in the "expected" way

My child enjoys playing with or doing the following with toys or objects:

throwing toys and objects onto the floor

My child can achieve his next play step by learning to imitate the following "expected" play action/s: throwing a ball into a laundry basket

This is his "opportunity."

What I will do first...

When my child is playing with a toy/object, I will:

- get down on the floor so we are face to face
- put the toy/s I plan to use beside me, with duplicates for my child
- **O**bserve what he is doing with the toy/s
- **W**ait to see what else he will do; and
- **L**isten to what he says

Then, I will R.O.C.K. my child's play...

I will Repeat (imitate) my child's actions with toys or objects.

When he does the following actions with toys/objects: throws them onto the floor, I will throw a toy or object onto the floor, using my own toy.

Once we have imitated each other back and forth a number of times...

I will then Repeat (model) the following new play step: throw a soft, small ball into a laundry basket

I will comment on the play action by saying: "I'm gonna throw the ball into the basket," or "The ball is in the basket!"

I will repeat the play step and comment 3 times in a row.

I will offer my child the opportunity to imitate the new play step (write down the new play step) Throwing the ball into the laundry basket

I will cue my child to imitate the play step by **waiting** for about 10 seconds.

If my child doesn't imitate the play step when I wait, I will provide a stronger cue by: Giving him hand over hand help so he throws a ball into the laundry basket

Once my child imitates the new play step (with or without a cue), I will reward him by: being excited and saying, "Yay! You threw the ball into the basket!"

I will not say, "Good job" or "Good boy."

I will **Keep the play fun** by: being playful, animated and making sure he is having fun

I will **Keep the play going** by: playing with him often using R.O.C.K., getting other family members to R.O.C.K. his play with the balls and the laundry basket and by introducing him to other throwing toys (bean bags, balls of different sizes) and different containers (garbage can, cardboard box).

My Child's Toy Play Plan

Complete this plan and use it to help your child learn to imitate the new play step.

My child is at the following stage of play: ______________________________

The next play step for my child is to: ______________________________

(For children at Exploring and Multi-action functional play stages)

My child will perform this play action by: ______________________________

____

My child enjoys playing with or doing the following with toys or objects:

____

My child can achieve his next play step by learning to imitate the following "expected" play action/s: ______________________________

This is his "opportunity."

What I will do first...

When my child is playing with a toy/object, I will:

- get down on the floor so we are face to face
- put the toy/s I plan to use beside me, with duplicates for my child
- **O**bserve what he is doing with the toy/s
- **W**ait to see what else he will do; and
- **L**isten to what he says

Then, I will R.O.C.K. my child's play...

R I will Repeat (imitate) my child's actions with toys or objects.

When he does the following actions with toys/objects: ____________________

________ , I will ______________________________ , using my own toy.

© Hanen Early Language Program, 2014.
This Toy Play Plan is from the Hanen guidebook *Take Out the Toys* (Sussman & Weitzman, 2014) and may be copied for personal use only.

Once we have imitated each other back and forth a number of times...

I will then Repeat (model) the following new play step: ____________________

____

I will comment on the play action by saying: ____________________

____

I will repeat the play step and comment ___ times in a row.

O I will offer my child the opportunity to imitate the new play step (write down the new play step) ____________________

____

C I will cue my child to imitate the play step by **waiting** for about ____ seconds.

If my child doesn't imitate the play step when I wait, I will provide a stronger cue by: ____________________

Once my child imitates the new play step (with or without a cue), I will reward him by: ____________________

I will not say, "Good job" or "Good boy."

K I will **Keep the play fun** by: ____________________

____

I will **Keep the play going** by: ____________________

____

____

© Hanen Early Language Program, 2014.
This Toy Play Plan is from the Hanen guidebook *Take Out the Toys* (Sussman & Weitzman, 2014) and may be copied for personal use only.